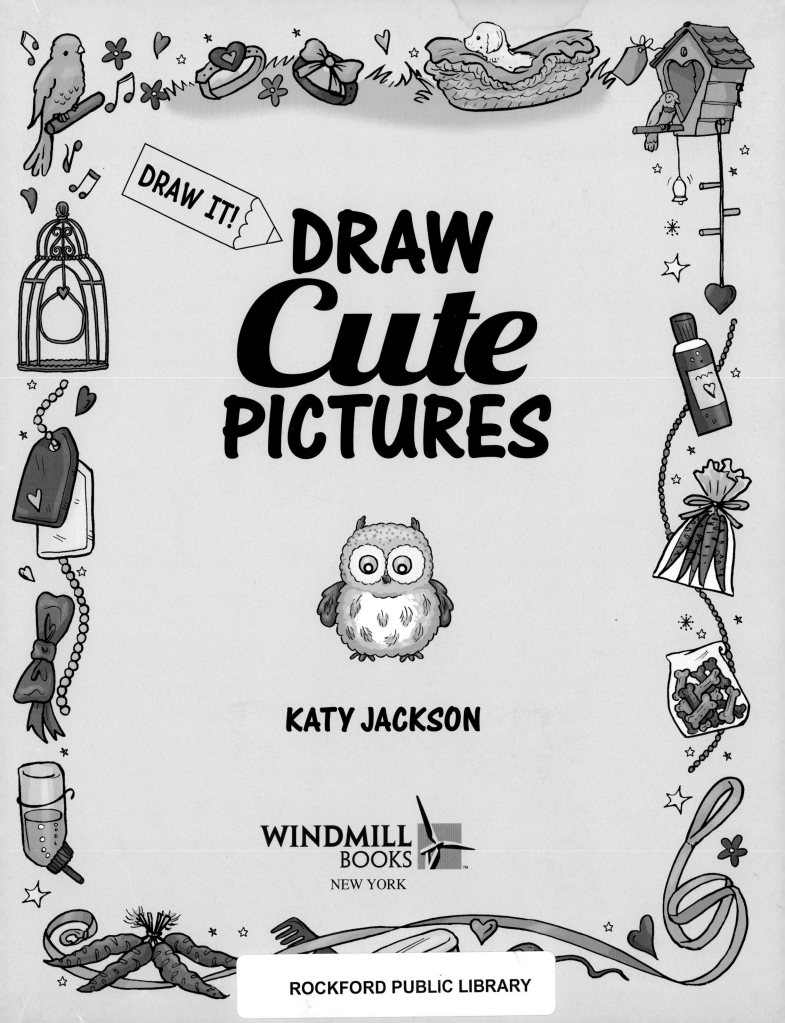

DRAW IT!

DRAW **Cute** PICTURES

KATY JACKSON

WINDMILL BOOKS
NEW YORK

Published in 2015 by Windmill Books, An Imprint of Rosen Publishing
29 East 21st Street, New York, NY 10010

First Edition

Text: Lisa Regan

Illustrations: Katy Jackson

Design: Notion Design

Editors: Joe Harris, Samantha Noonan, and Samantha Hilton

With thanks to Frances Evans and Jessica Williams

US editor: Joshua Shadowens

Library of Congress Cataloging-in-Publication Data

Jackson, Katy (Katy E.)

Draw cute pictures / By Katy Jackson. -- First Edition.

   pages cm. -- (Draw it!)

Includes index.

ISBN 978-1-4777-9132-5 (library binding) -- ISBN 978-1-4777-9133-2
(pbk.) -- ISBN 978-1-4777-9134-9 (6-pack)

1. Characters and characteristics in art--Juvenile literature.
2. Drawing--Technique--Juvenile literature. I. Title.

NC825.C43J333 2015

741.2--dc23

2014008388

Printed in the United States

SL004210US

CPSIA Compliance Information: Batch #AS4102WM: For Further Information contact Windmill Books, New York, New York at 1-866-478-0556

Contents

Getting Started

This book will teach you how to draw a cast of wonderful characters. Simply follow the step-by-step instructions, and get drawing!

1. Start with a plain piece of unlined paper. If you are going to paint your picture, you should use thick paper.

2. Use a pencil to copy the step-by-step instructions. Soft pencils are good for rough sketches. Hard pencils are best for details.

3. Draw over your pencil lines with a black pen or a thin brush and black ink. The ink must be waterproof if you are going to add watercolor paints to your picture.

INK

4. When the pen ink has dried, use a large, soft eraser to remove the rough pencil marks. Now your picture is looking nice and neat!

5. Complete your picture by coloring it in with colored felt-tip pens, pencils, or paint.

6. Paintbrushes come in different shapes. When painting, use a thin, pointed brush for detail and a fatter brush for flat areas of color.

Fizzy the Pony

1. Draw two circles side by side for Fizzy's body. Add his head slightly to the right, like an upside-down teardrop.

2. Connect these shapes with curved lines. Fizzy is coming to life already!

3. Erase the lines you don't need. Draw in his legs with simple lines. The front legs are straight, but the back legs bend backward. Add four hoof shapes.

4. Use your guide lines to help you fill out his legs. They need to be wider at the top.

5. Draw in a thick mane and tail. Don't forget his ears and the forelock in between them. Show Fizzy's cute character with a small eye, mouth, and nostrils.

6. Finally, give Fizzy some fluffy fur around his hooves and a pattern on his coat. Erase any spare lines, and finish his mane and tail. Use different shades of brown to color in his fur.

Cleo the Cat

1. Cleo starts out as two ovals. The smaller one should be tilted slightly.

2. Sketch little lines to show where her tail and legs will go. Remember, she's a dainty little kitty!

3. Make her face the right shape by drawing in two triangles for ears and a little pointed chin underneath.

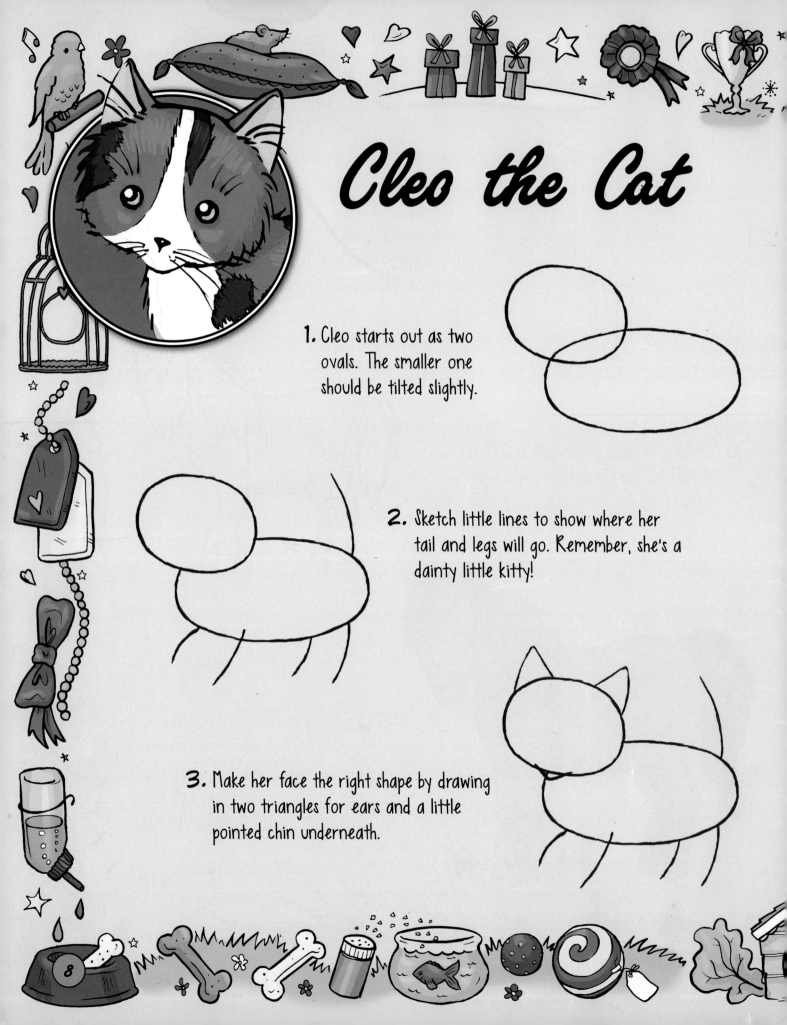

4. Add two circles for her eyes, then add a little nose. Make her legs and tail wider, following your lines.

5. Erase any lines you don't need. Add detail to her ears, eyes, and paws. Draw in rough patterns on her fur.

6. Fluff her up with little pencil lines around the edge of her body, and don't forget to draw her whiskers. Shade in her fur with pretty colors. Now she's purr-fect!

Squeaky the Guinea Pig

1. Start by drawing a soft, curved triangle for Squeaky's head.

2. Add her body by drawing a large oval. The side of the oval should overlap the head by more than half.

3. Draw two cute little feet at the front and one at the back. She has four feet, of course, but one is hidden in this picture!

4. Sketch in her sweet little face, complete with a snuffling nose. Don't forget her wiggly ears!

5. Erase the top of her head and replace it with some tufty fur on top. Fill in her eye, and add a few little whiskers and dots.

6. Use short pencil strokes to make her fur look more fluffy. Use the same strokes to add a pattern on her back, too. Then use honey colors to create her lovely fur. On your marks, get set, SQUEAK!

Barney the Pup

1. Draw a circle for Barney's head and an oval underneath, but overlapping, for his body.

2. Sketch lines to show where his front legs and paws will go. Add a sausage on each side to start his back legs.

3. Two triangles make his floppy ears, then sketch in the start of his waggly tail! Maybe he is hoping for a treat?

4. Start to draw his cute puppy face. His mouth is two curves. Make his front legs wider.

5. Barney is a panting pup, so draw in his tongue! Then add some fluffy tufts on top of his head.

6. Finally, make him look furry by adding rough lines all around the edges of your drawing. Make his ears rounder and his tail fatter. Choose your favorite pencil to color in Barney's fur. Woof, woof!

Belle the Little Dog

1. Draw a shape like a fat number eight. This will be Belle's face and the front part of her body.

2. Give her two little triangular ears. Draw her eyes and nose and a wide, curved mouth. She's such a happy dog!

3. Draw her eyebrows and a tongue sticking out of her mouth. Add a circle for the back of her body.

4. Use lines to show where her curved tail will be and also her four legs. Her back legs are bent. Add four circles for her paws.

5. Give her a big, fluffy tail with lots of pencil strokes following the guide line. Make her legs wider.

6. Now fluff out her body and face, so that she's a big bundle of fur. Then begin to shade in her fur with a pretty color. Draw her a special bow, and she's all ready to greet the customers!

Greta the Squirrel

1. First, draw Greta's head. It is a triangle with rounded corners.

2. Add a teardrop-shaped body. Sketch two little lines to show where her legs and arms will go.

3. Work on the legs and arms to make them fatter and more shapely. She's sitting neatly, ready to go acorn hunting!

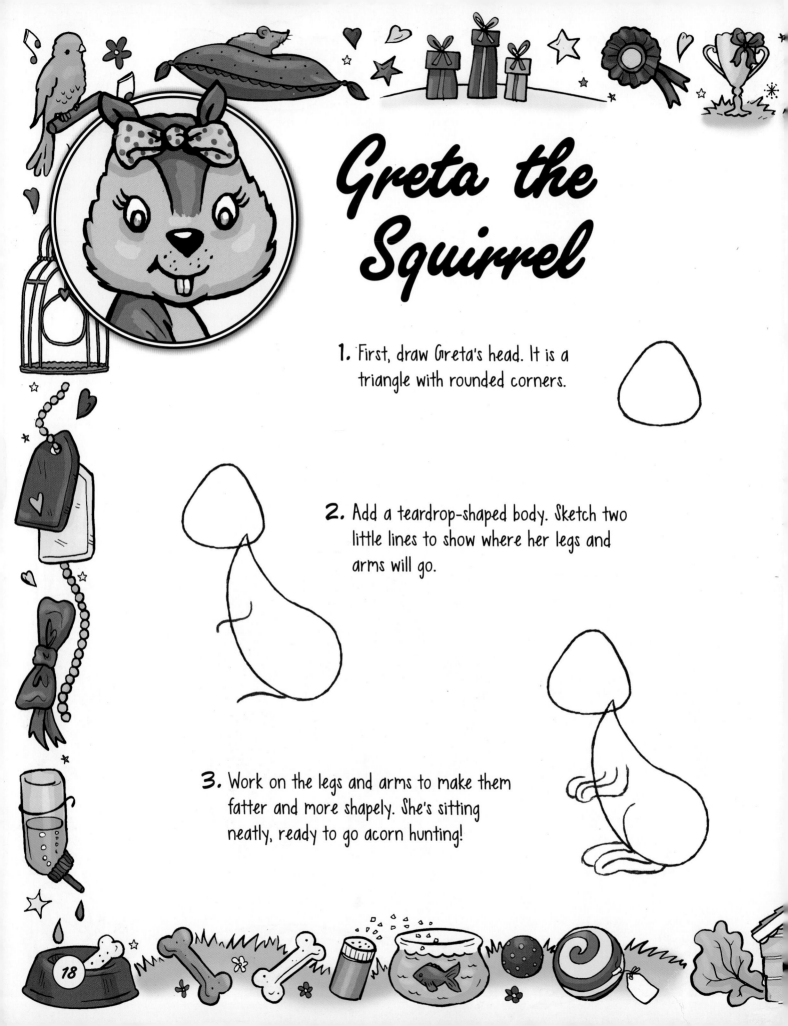

4. Erase your guide lines, and then add in her little squirrel face. She's starting to look really cute!

5. Draw her ears and front teeth. Add a large tail, like a backward comma. Fluff out her chest with some extra fur.

6. Make her tail wonderfully big and bushy, and add fluffy pencil lines all around for her fur. Color in her body, and draw a cute, colorful bow on her head. She's off to play with her friends now!

Zachary the Bunny

1. Carefully draw three circles all linked together, like this. He looks a little like a caterpillar at this stage!

2. Join the lower circles to make Zachary's body, and add a little nose shape on his face.

3. Sketch the shape of his ears, and draw some cute paws. Now he looks more like a bunny rabbit!

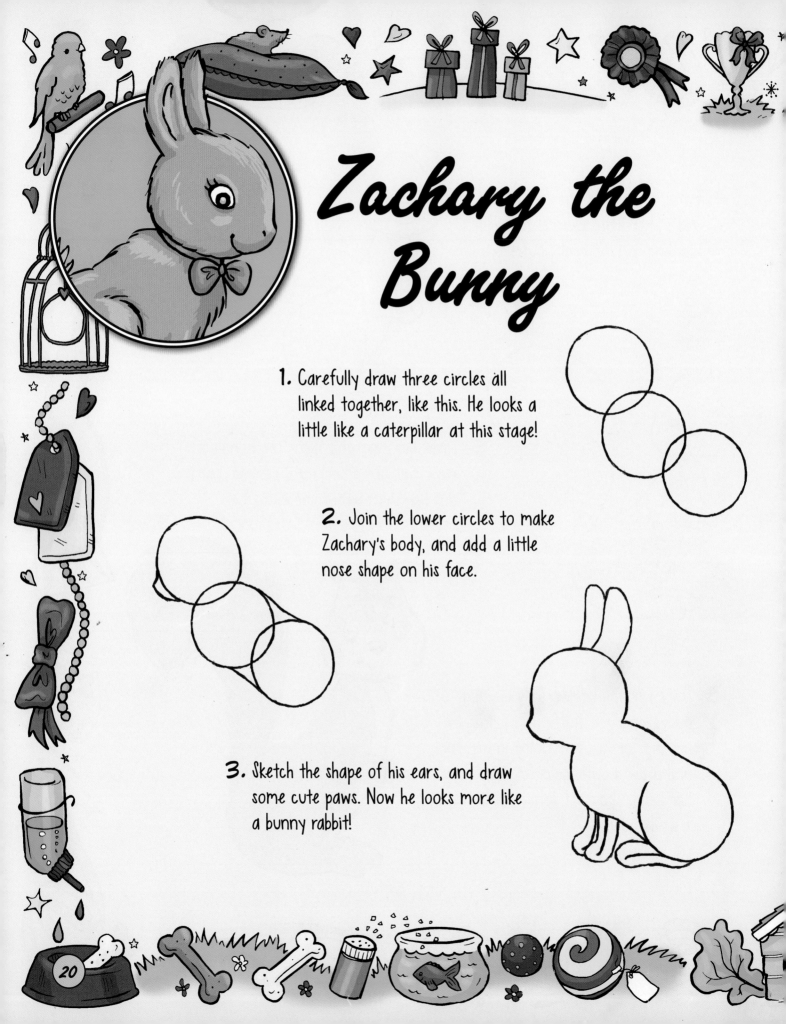

4. Erase the lines you don't need. Draw his face with a big oval eye, and add a fluffy tail on his bottom.

5. Fill in the detail on his eye. It won't be long before he is ready to hop off the page!

6. Finish with his trademark bow tie, and add lots of extra lines to fluff him up around the edges. Color him in so he looks like a real bunny!

Egbert the Owl

1. Egbert starts life as a fat, slightly squashed circle. This will be his head.

2. Draw the same shape, but slightly bigger, underneath. They should overlap each other.

3. Erase the overlapping line, then add two huge eyes. This is so that Egbert can see well in the dark.

4. Draw two frilly circles around the outside of his eyes, then add his beak.

5. Finish his eyes, then add feathery ears and wings. Draw in his little three-toed feet, so he can sit on his branch.

6. Erase the dividing line and draw a small chin. Fill in his body with a combination of colors, then add some downy feathers to make him a real bundle of fluff!

Amelie the Fawn

1. Start by drawing her body. It's the shape of a jelly bean! Add a circle for her head, a little off to the right.

2. Sketch four bent lines to show where her legs will go. She needs them to trot around the forest.

3. Develop her legs so they're the right shape, and add hooves. Connect her head with a curved neck, and draw a pointed snout at the front of her face.

4. Erase all the guide lines so that you can see Amelie's body taking shape. Sketch her perky little tail and two pricked-up ears.

5. Amelie's huge eye is shaped like a leaf. Add it in, and mark her mouth and nostril.

6. Finish her with the stripe along her head and down her back. Pick some woodland colors to shade in all of her lovely fur. What a pretty girl she is!

Jackson the Cub

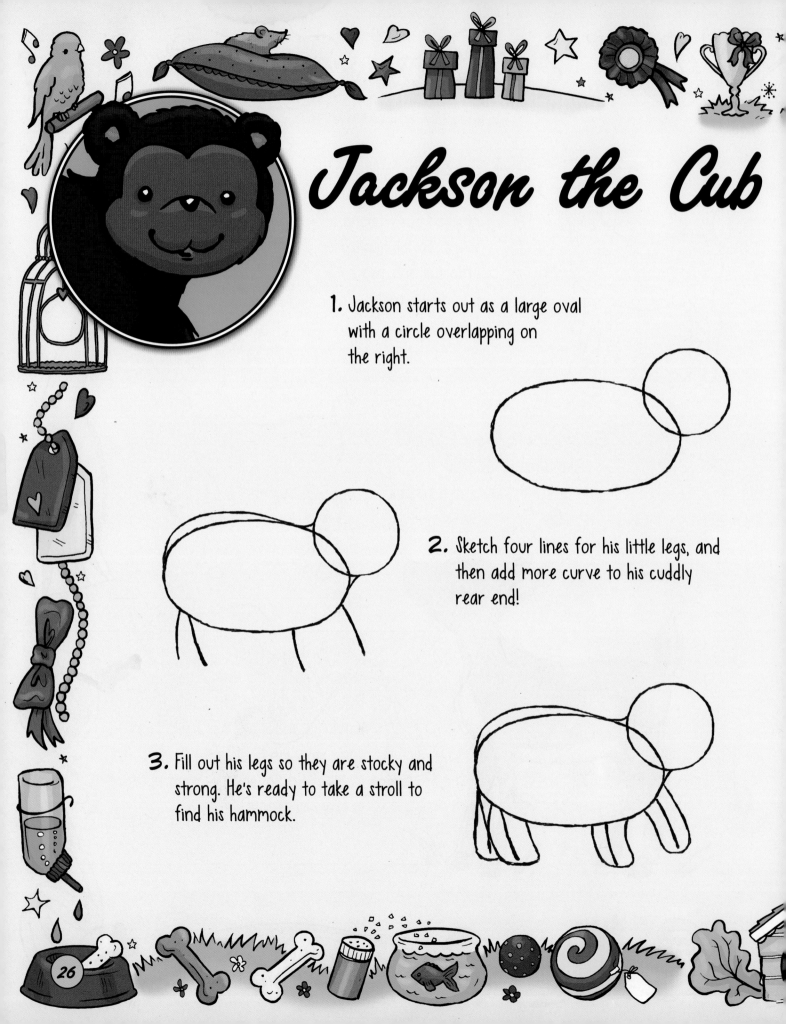

1. Jackson starts out as a large oval with a circle overlapping on the right.

2. Sketch four lines for his little legs, and then add more curve to his cuddly rear end!

3. Fill out his legs so they are stocky and strong. He's ready to take a stroll to find his hammock.

4. Add two round ears and a little fluffy tail. Now you can erase your guide lines. He looks like a real teddy bear!

5. Draw his eyes, nose, and mouth. Add lines to show where the fur on his face changes shade.

6. Have fun making him all furry with rough pencil strokes, and add his paw pads. Color in all his thick and fluffy fur. Now he's the cuddliest bear in the forest!

Sammy the Seal

1. Draw a circle, then add two semicircles on the lower edge to make Sammy's chubby little cheeks.

2. Add a leaf shape for his body. The end almost completely overlaps his head. This shape helps him to be a great swimmer.

3. Erase the lines you don't need. Draw in curved lines to show Sammy's flippers and tail.

4. Draw two large circular eyes, halfway down his face. Add a curve over his nose and two curves for his mouth. Make his flippers the right shape.

5. Finish his eyes, and add a V-shaped nose and cute little eyebrows.

6. Complete Sammy with some whiskers, and add some rough lines to make his body furry. Choose a color for his fur, then shade in his body. He's all ready to swim away!

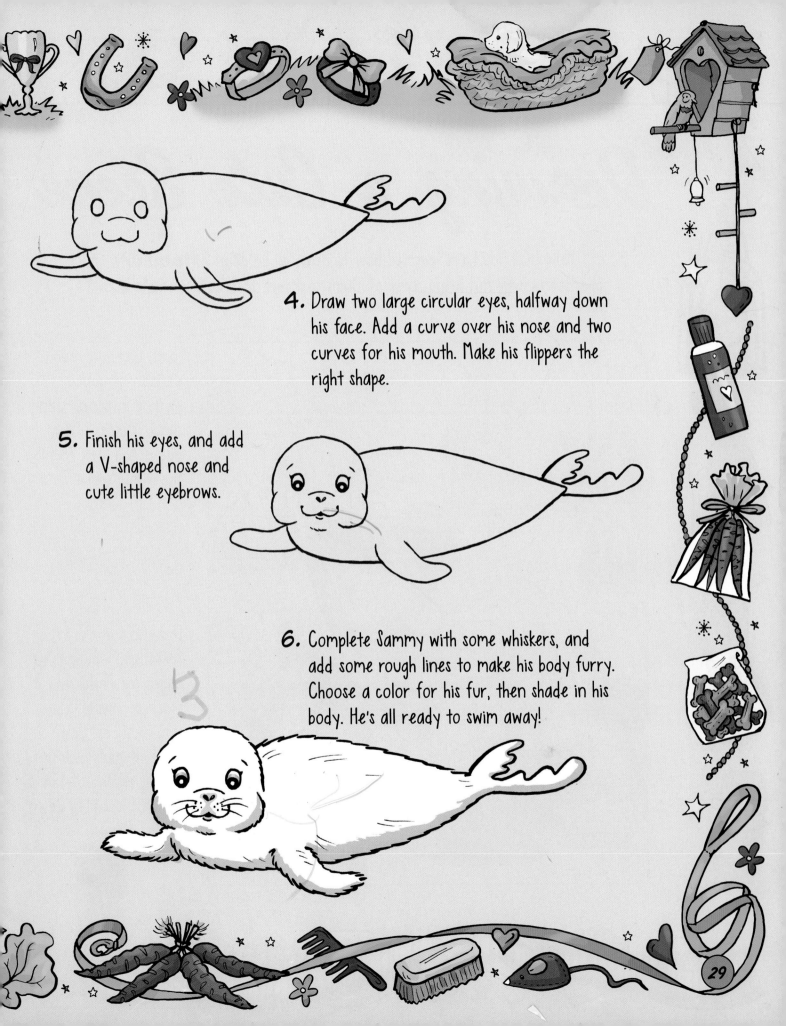

Drawing a Cute Scene

Now that you have learned how to draw all kinds of different cute characters, why not bring some of them together to create a whole scene?

1

First, sketch a rough version of your picture in pencil, using simple shapes. Then add detail. Try to fill the whole space.

Draw in some pretty furniture, hanging cages for birds, and stacked objects. That way, you can show some animals high up sitting on top of things, while others play down on the floor.

Now it's time to add some color! Think about which shades work well together and how they make you feel.

Yellow is a friendly, happy color. That's why we chose it for the wall in the background. It makes the whole picture feel cheerful and fresh.

We have colored the furniture in brighter colors than the background. This helps it to stand out!

It's a good idea to use lots of different colors if you want to create a sense of energy and excitement.

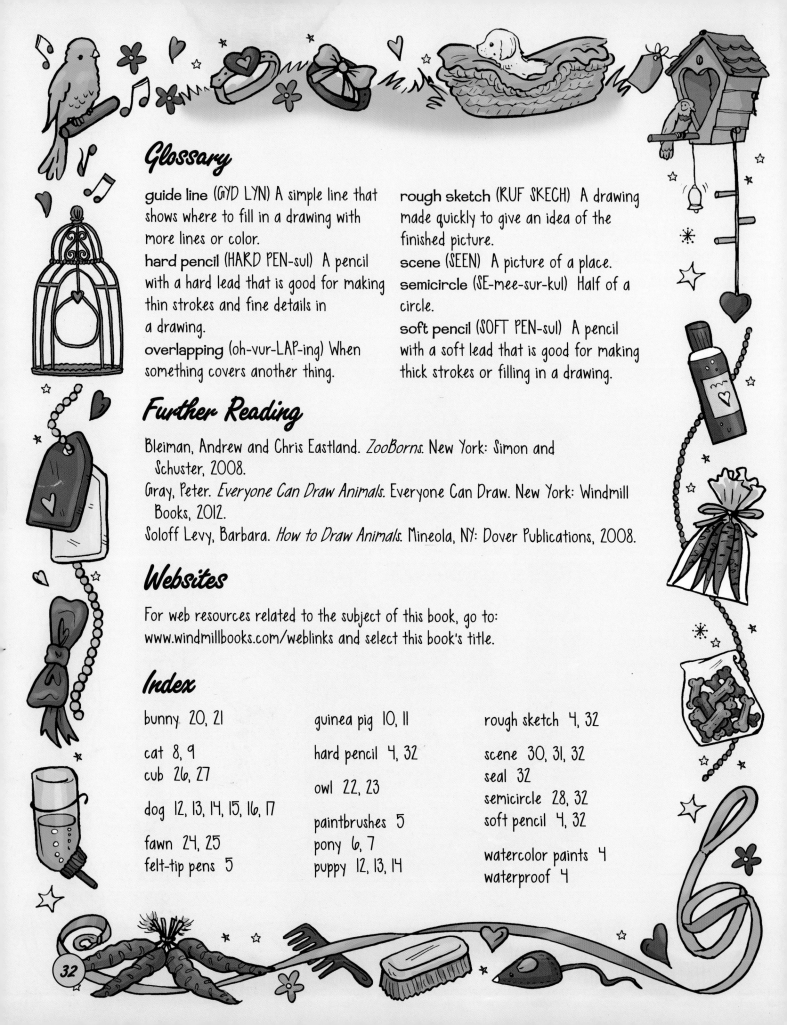

Glossary

guide line (GYD LYN) A simple line that shows where to fill in a drawing with more lines or color.

hard pencil (HARD PEN-sul) A pencil with a hard lead that is good for making thin strokes and fine details in a drawing.

overlapping (oh-vur-LAP-ing) When something covers another thing.

rough sketch (RUF SKECH) A drawing made quickly to give an idea of the finished picture.

scene (SEEN) A picture of a place.

semicircle (SE-mee-sur-kul) Half of a circle.

soft pencil (SOFT PEN-sul) A pencil with a soft lead that is good for making thick strokes or filling in a drawing.

Further Reading

Bleiman, Andrew and Chris Eastland. *ZooBorns.* New York: Simon and Schuster, 2008.

Gray, Peter. *Everyone Can Draw Animals.* Everyone Can Draw. New York: Windmill Books, 2012.

Soloff Levy, Barbara. *How to Draw Animals.* Mineola, NY: Dover Publications, 2008.

Websites

For web resources related to the subject of this book, go to: www.windmillbooks.com/weblinks and select this book's title.

Index